Junior Great Books®

D1551083

Reader's Journal

Series 3   Book Two

This book belongs to:

_____

The Great Books Foundation
A nonprofit educational organization

The interpretive discussion program that moves
students toward excellence in reading comprehension,
critical thinking, and writing

Junior Great Books® is a registered trademark of the Great Books Foundation. Shared Inquiry™ is a trademark of the Great Books Foundation. The contents of this publication include proprietary trademarks and copyrighted materials, and may be used or quoted only with permission and appropriate credit to the Foundation.

Copyright © 2006 by The Great Books Foundation
Chicago, Illinois
All rights reserved
ISBN 1-933147-27-X

First printing
9 8 7 6 5 4 3 2 1
Printed in the United States of America

Cover art by Vivienne Flesher. Copyright © 2006 by Vivienne Flesher.
Text and cover design by William Seabright, William Seabright & Associates.
Interior design by Think Design Group.

Published and distributed by

The Great Books Foundation
A nonprofit educational organization
35 East Wacker Drive, Suite 2300
Chicago, IL 60601-2205

Welcome to Your Reader's Journal

This Reader's Journal is a place for you to collect your thoughts about the Junior Great Books stories you read and discuss in class. Here, you can also be an artist and a poet, while discovering some secrets to becoming a strong reader and writer.

There are many parts of the Reader's Journal to explore:

Writing Notebook allows you to gather some of your favorite pieces of writing in one place to revise and polish them.

Curious Words is where you can record the strange or interesting words you come across while reading. You don't have to memorize these words—you get to play with them, sounding them out in your head or out loud or using them to make up messages and rhymes.

The **glossary** contains unusual or difficult words from the stories you've read. Look here for definitions that will help you better understand what you are reading.

Are you hunting for a **keeper question**, or do you have your **Head in the Clouds**? Maybe you're **Building Your Answer**, **Writing to Explain** or **Explore**, or getting **Into Reading**. Whatever you're working on, this Reader's Journal belongs to you. It's the place for your great ideas.

Contents

The Dream Weaver

Concha Castroviejo

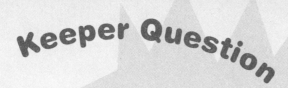

Keeper Question

In the space below, write a **keeper question** about the story that came into your mind during the first reading, while sharing questions, or even right now. Choose a question that no one has completely answered yet, and keep it in your mind during the second reading. If you still have the question after reading, continue to think about it—you picked a real keeper!

Your keeper question:

_____

_____

_____

_____

Into Reading
Making Inferences

Inferences can help you figure out things that are not directly stated in the story. To make an inference, you combine clues in the story with your own ideas.

- Read the passage and question below.

- Write your answer to the question.

- Circle word clues in the passage that helped you make the inference to answer the question.

Passage (pages 17–18)

Little by little, Rogelia learned to make lovely woven fabrics of the color and shape of clouds. She learned how to make the rainbow tarry by singing to it, and how to wrap it up in orange-colored dreams. She learned to weave pink and blue dreams for the young, and green ones to console those who were sick and those who were sad. And white dreams so that children could embroider them in color.

"You're a very clever little girl," old Gosvinda told her.

Question: Does Rogelia enjoy her work with Gosvinda?

Your answer:

_____

_____

_____

_____

Head in the Clouds

Use your imagination! Choose one of the topics in the clouds and draw a picture or write a little more about the story.

My favorite part of the story

A picture of Rogelia's weaving

Some thoughts about my keeper question

An occupation I would be good at

Building Your Answer

The focus question:

_____

_____

_____

_____

Your answer before the discussion:

_____

_____

_____

_____

Your answer after the discussion (you may change or add to your first answer):

_____

_____

_____

_____

_____

_____

Prewriting Notes

Complete the character web on the next page by writing words that describe Rogelia in the boxes. Base your description on what is in the story.

Near each box, write one or two sentences about why you chose the word in the box. Use evidence from the story to support your answer.

A **character** is someone in a story, play, or poem. **Character traits** tell what a character looks like, says, and does. They also tell how a character feels about people or things and how a character seems to other characters.

Writing to Explain
Writing About Character

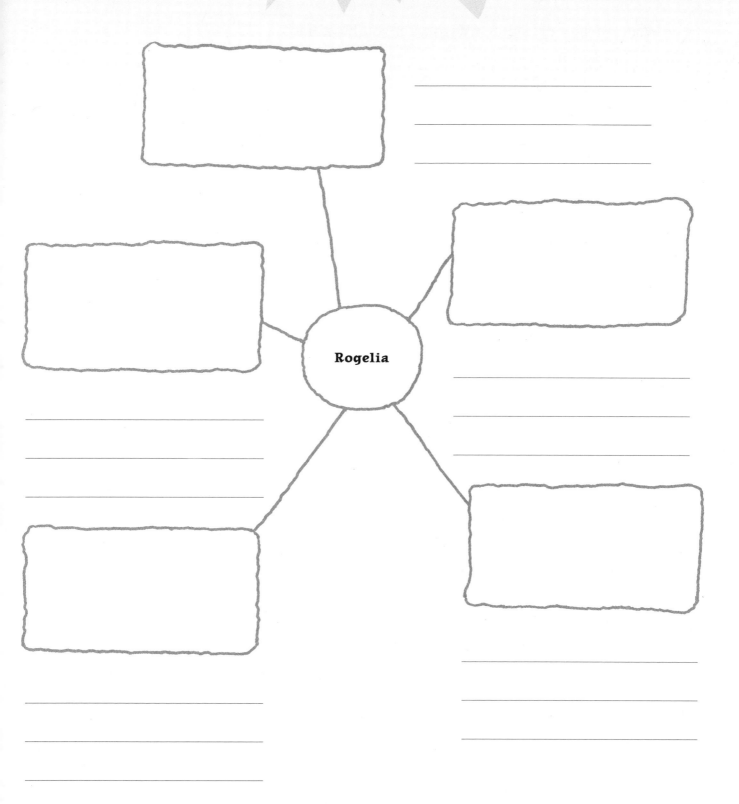

Rogelia

Writing to Explore
Dream Weaving

Prewriting Notes

Write about a dream or a daydream you have had.

An interesting or exciting part of your dream:

_____

_____

Details about what you saw, heard, smelled, tasted, and touched:

I saw _____

_____

I heard _____

_____

I smelled or tasted _____

_____

I touched _____

_____

How you felt in the dream:

_____

_____

_____

Writing a Draft

My Dream

_____

_____

_____

_____

_____

_____

_____

_____

_____

_____

Jean Labadie's Big Black Dog

French-Canadian folktale as told by Natalie Savage Carlson

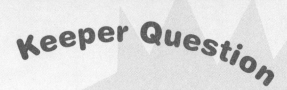

Keeper Question

In the space below, write a keeper question about the story that came into your mind during the first reading, while sharing questions, or even right now. Choose a question that no one has completely answered yet, and keep it in your mind during the second reading. If you still have the question after reading, continue to think about it—you picked a real keeper!

Your keeper question:

_____

_____

_____

_____

Into Reading

Making Inferences

Inferences can help you figure out things that are not directly stated in the story. To make an inference, you combine clues in the story with your own ideas.

- Read the following passage and question.

- Write your answer to the question.

- Circle word clues in the passage that helped you make the inference to answer the question.

- Write down your own ideas that helped you make the inference.

Passage (pages 27–28)

"Have you seen my big black dog, André?" he asked his neighbor.

"What big black dog?" asked André. "I didn't know you had a dog."

"I just got him from the Indians," said Jean. "Someone has been stealing my chickens so I got myself a dog to protect them. He is a very fierce dog, bigger than a wolf and twice as wild."

Continue ⟶

Into Reading

Making Inferences

Question: What does Jean Labadie want André to think of the big black dog?

Your answer:

_____

_____

_____

_____

Your own ideas that helped you make the inference:

_____

_____

_____

_____

Head in the Clouds

Use your imagination! Choose one of the topics in the clouds and draw a picture or write a little more about the story.

A picture of the big black dog

My favorite character in the story, and why

Something in the story that I'm still wondering about

A note to André Drouillard

Building Your Answer

The focus question:

_____

_____

_____

Your answer before the discussion:

_____

_____

_____

Your answer after the discussion *(you may change or add to your first answer):*

_____

_____

_____

_____

_____

A part of the story that helps support your answer:

_____

_____

_____

_____

Writing to Explain
Problems and Solutions

Prewriting Notes

With a partner, write Jean Labadie's problems and solutions in the order they happen in the story.

> A story **problem** happens when someone or something is working against a story character.
>
> A story **solution** happens when someone or something fixes the problem.

Jean Labadie

Problem #1	Solution #1
_____	_____
_____	_____
_____	_____
_____	_____

Problem #2	Solution #2
_____	_____
_____	_____
_____	_____
_____	_____

Problem #3

_____

_____

_____

_____

_____

Solution #3

_____

_____

_____

_____

_____

Problem #4

_____

_____

_____

_____

_____

Solution #4

_____

_____

_____

_____

_____

Problem #5

_____

_____

_____

_____

_____

Solution #5

_____

_____

_____

_____

_____

Writing to Explore
Great Storytellers

Prewriting Notes

When I saw the *loup-garou*, it was a _____ !

Some important features:

The *loup-garou* has _____

_____

_____

_____

It looks like _____

_____

It sounds like _____

_____

It smells like _____

_____

It lives in _____

_____

It eats _____

_____

Writing to Explore
Great Storytellers

Writing a Draft

Look Out for the *Loup-Garou!*

When I saw the *loup-garou*, it was a _____ !

_____

_____

_____

_____

_____

_____

_____

_____

_____

_____

_____

The Loup-Garou

Caporushes

English folktale as told by Flora Annie Steel

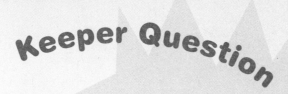

Keeper Question

In the space below, write a keeper question about the story that came into your mind during the first reading, while sharing questions, or even right now. Choose a question that no one has completely answered yet, and keep it in your mind during the second reading. If you still have the question after reading, continue to think about it—you picked a real keeper!

Your keeper question:

_____

_____

_____

_____

Into Reading

Making Inferences

Inferences can help you figure out things that are not directly stated in the story. To make an inference, you combine clues in the story with your own ideas.

- Read the following passage and question below.

- Write your answer to the question.

- Circle word clues in the passage that helped you make the inference to answer the question.

- Write down your own ideas that helped you make the inference.

Passage (pages 54–55)

Then the old man sobbed, "I had a daughter whom I loved dearly, dearly. And I asked her how much she loved me, and she replied, 'As fresh meat loves salt.' And I was angry with her and turned her out of house and home, for I thought she didn't love me at all. But now I see she loved me best of all."

Continue ⟶

Question: How does the father feel about turning his daughter out of the house?

Your answer:

_____

_____

_____

_____

Your own ideas that helped you make the inference:

_____

_____

_____

_____

Head in the Clouds

Use your imagination! Choose one of the topics in the clouds and draw a picture or write a little more about the story.

My favorite part of the story

A picture of my favorite character

How dancing makes me feel

A note to Caporushes' father

Building Your Answer

The focus question:

_____

_____

_____

Your answer before the discussion:

_____

_____

_____

Your answer after the discussion (you may change or add to your first answer):

_____

_____

_____

An answer you heard during the discussion that was different from yours:

_____

_____

_____

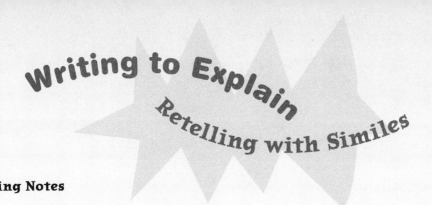

Writing to Explain
Retelling with Similes

Prewriting Notes

Look at the example below. Then complete the similes to describe parts of the story. For each simile, find a phrase or sentence from the story that helped you write it. Then explain your simile.

> A **simile** is a poetic comparison using the word **like** or **as**. For example, "Her smile is like the sun" or "The wind was as quiet as a whisper."

Caporushes' father's anger is / like \ a tornado.

Explanation: "So there and then he turned her out of the home where she had been born and bred, and shut the door in her face."

Caporushes' father's anger is like a tornado, because they are both wild and come up suddenly.
Page: 41

Caporushes and the Prince dance / like \ .

Explanation: _____

_____

_____

Page: _____

Writing to Explain
Retelling with Similes

The scullery maid works as hard / as _____ .

Explanation: _____

_____

_____

_____ **Page:** _____

Caporushes is as clever / as _____ .

Explanation: _____

_____

_____

_____ **Page:** _____

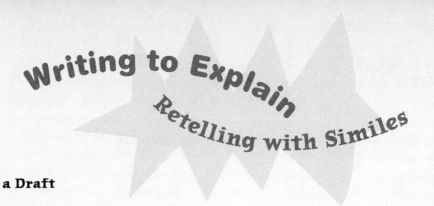

Writing a Draft

In the space below, write the story of "Caporushes" in your own words, using the similes you wrote.

_____

_____

_____

_____

_____

_____

_____

_____

_____

_____

_____

_____

_____

_____

_____

_____

Writing to Explain
Retelling with Similes

Use this page if you need more room.

_____

_____

_____

_____

_____

_____

_____

_____

_____

_____

_____

_____

_____

_____

_____

Writing to Explore
Have You Seen Caporushes?

Prewriting Notes

Go back through the story and find some words or phrases describing Caporushes. Write them in the boxes below. Then make up your own simile from each description.

Description of Caporushes	"beautiful golden hair" Page: 42
Simile	Her hair is / like \ a sunflower.

Description of Caporushes	Page:
Simile	

Description of Caporushes	Page:
Simile	

Writing a Draft

Write your own description of Caporushes below, using the similes you created, and draw a picture of her to go with your description.

HAVE YOU SEEN THIS PERSON?

_____

_____

_____

_____

_____

_____

_____

_____

_____

_____

_____

_____

If you have seen her, please tell the master's son!

The Upside-Down Boy

Juan Felipe Herrera

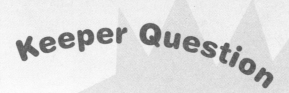

Keeper Question

In the space below, write down as your keeper question one of the interpretive questions you talked about in class. Then answer the question at the bottom of the page.

Your keeper question:

_____

_____

_____

_____

How did you decide to choose this question?

_____

_____

_____

_____

When you read, you decide which details are most important in helping you understand the story's main ideas or themes.

Read the passage below from the story.

Passage (page 64)

I pop up shaking. I am
    alone facing the class.

"Ready to sing?" Mrs. Sampson
    asks me.

I am frozen, then a deep
    breath fills me,

"Three blind mice, three
    blind mice," I sing.

My eyes open as big as the ceiling, and
my hands spread out as if catching
raindrops from the sky.

Continue ⟶

Into Reading
Determining Important Ideas

Below the example, write down some important words or phrases in the passage, what they mean in your own words, and the reason you think they are important. Look at the example if you need help.

Example

Some important words or phrases in this passage: *I pop up shaking. I am alone facing the class.*

What these words or phrases mean (in your own words): *Juanito is worried that he can't sing the song.*

The reason you think this part of the passage is important: *It tells us how he feels about being new and not knowing the language.*

Some important words or phrases in this passage:

_____

_____

_____

What these words or phrases mean (in your own words):

_____

_____

_____

The reason you think this part of the passage is important:

_____

_____

_____

Head in the Clouds

Use your imagination! Choose one of the topics in the clouds and draw a picture or write a little more about the story.

My favorite
character
in the story

Something
Juanito's
poem makes
me think of

A sentence
from the story
that I liked,
and why

time when
I felt upside down

Building Your Answer

The focus question:

_____

_____

_____

_____

Your answer before the discussion:

_____

_____

_____

_____

Your answer after the discussion (you may change or add to your first answer):

_____

_____

_____

_____

_____

Writing to Explain
Feeling Upside Down

Find three examples of imagery in "The Upside-Down Boy" that help you understand Juanito and some of his thoughts and feelings. Below, write the imagery from the story and what it tells you about Juanito.

> **Imagery** is language that creates a picture in the reader's mind. Examples of imagery: "Will my tongue turn into a rock?" (page 58), "The school bell rings and shakes me," (page 61) or "Tomato cars and cucumber sombreros" (page 60).

Imagery on page _____ : _____

_____

What it tells you about Juanito: _____

_____

_____

Imagery on page _____ : _____

_____

What it tells you about Juanito: _____

_____

_____

Imagery on page _____ : _____

_____

What it tells you about Juanito: _____

_____

_____

Writing a Draft

In the space below, draft your essay to answer the following question:
How does the imagery in "The Upside-Down Boy" help you understand Juanito? Give your essay a title that will get the reader's attention about your topic.

_____

_____

_____

_____

_____

_____

_____

_____

_____

_____

_____

_____

_____

_____

_____

Writing to Explain
Feeling Upside Down

Use this page if you need more room.

_____

_____

_____

_____

_____

_____

_____

_____

_____

_____

_____

_____

_____

_____

_____

_____

_____

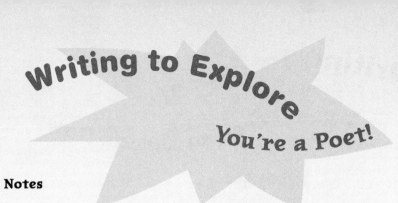

Writing to Explore

You're a Poet!

Prewriting Notes

Choose two words, one from each list, that go together in some way.

At School	In Nature
Eraser	River
Bell	Desert
Hallway	Crow
Homework	Rainstorm
Blackboard	Stone

Your own words:

_____

_____

_____

Your own words:

_____

_____

_____

Explain how the two words you chose are alike.

_____

_____

_____

_____

_____

_____

Writing to Explore
You're a Poet!

Now practice making a **metaphor** with your two words.

For example: *My eraser is a rainstorm.*

Your metaphor:

The / My _____ is a _____ .

> A **metaphor** is a statement or sentence that compares two things **without** using the words *like* or *as*.
>
> For example: "My tongue is a rock." ("The Upside-Down Boy," page 60)

To write the second line of your poem, write a short sentence using a verb (an action word) to show how your metaphor makes sense.

For example: *It washes away my mistakes.*

_____

Writing a Draft

Write the two lines of your poem below. Add more to your poem if you wish.

_____

_____

_____

_____

_____

_____

The Green Man

Gail E. Haley

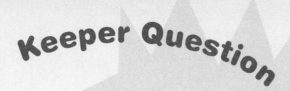

Keeper Question

In the space below, write down as your keeper question one of the interpretive questions you talked about in class. Then write down some of the parts of the story that relate to your keeper question.

Your keeper question:

_____

_____

_____

_____

Write down some parts of the story that have something to do with your keeper question.

_____

_____

_____

_____

_____

_____

Into Reading
Determining Important Ideas

When you read, you decide which details are most important in helping you understand the story's main ideas or themes.

Read the passage below from the story. Then fill out the chart that follows.

Passage (pages 78 and 79)

One morning, after a heavy rainstorm, Claude heard a frantic bellow coming from the direction of the river. He hurried there to see what was wrong, and found a cow who had been separated from her calf. They had taken shelter from the rain in a hilltop thicket, and as the water rose the river had surrounded them, turning the hillock into an island. The terrified calf would not follow its mother through the swirling current, and the cow was mooing loudly for help.

Claude waded across the water, picked up the calf, and carried it to its mother. Gratefully, the cow licked his hand and then led her calf away through the forest toward the safety of the farmyard.

Continue ⟶

Into Reading
Determining Important Ideas

Below the example, write down some important words or phrases in this passage, what they mean in your own words, and the reason you think they are important. Look at the example if you need help.

Some important words or details in this passage

Claude hears a frantic bellow.

Into Reading
Determining Important Ideas

What these words or details mean (in your own words)	The reason you think these words or details are important
Claude thinks an animal might need help.	It shows Claude cares about living things.

Head in the Clouds

Use your imagination! Choose one of the topics in the clouds and draw a picture or write a little more about the story.

My favorite
part of
the story

What
it looks like
inside
Claude's
cave

Why I would
be good at taking
the place of
the Green Man

Some thoughts about
my keeper question

Building Your Answer

The focus question:

_____

_____

_____

Your answer before the discussion:

_____

_____

_____

Your answer after the discussion _(you may change or add to your first answer):_

_____

_____

_____

Two pieces of evidence from the story that support your answer:

1. _____

_____

_____

2. _____

_____

_____

Writing to Explain
Story Setting

Prewriting Notes

Complete the chart below. In the column on the left, describe the different settings in "The Green Man." In the column on the right, explain how Claude behaves and feels in each setting. Remember to look back through the story to help you complete the chart.

> The **setting** is the time and place of a story.

A setting in "The Green Man"	How Claude behaves and feels in that setting
An expensive restaurant in the village	Claude is arrogant, vain, and selfish. He makes fun of the people putting food out for the Green Man.

Writing to Explain
Story Setting

Writing a Draft

Now write an essay answering this question: **How does living in the forest change Claude?** Use your prewriting notes, and give your essay an interesting title.

_____

_____

_____

What is the setting at first?	_____
	_____

What is Claude like in this setting?	_____
	_____

How does the setting change? How does Claude change?	_____
	_____

_____

_____

_____

Writing to Explain
Story Setting

Use this page if you need more room.

_____

_____

_____

_____

_____

_____

_____

_____

_____

_____

_____

_____

_____

_____

_____

_____

_____

_____

_____

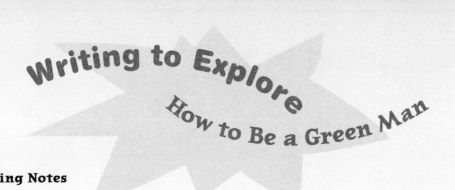

Writing to Explore
How to Be a Green Man

Prewriting Notes

Write down something Claude does to become the Green Man. In the left-hand column, write down some ideas about how to do that thing, using details from the story and from your imagination. Then, number each step in the order you want it to appear in your instructions.

Something Claude does: _____

How to do it:	Order:

Writing to Explore
How to Be a Green Man

Writing a Draft

Write a set of instructions for the next Green Man to complete the task you chose. Write each step in order and be as clear as possible so the Green Man knows just what to do.

Instructions for the Next Green Man

How to _____ :

First, _____

_____

_____

Then, _____

_____

_____

Then, _____

_____

_____

Then, _____

_____

_____

The Ugly Duckling

Hans Christian Andersen

Keeper Question

In the space below, write down as your keeper question one of the interpretive questions you talked about in class. Then write down some parts of the story that relate to your keeper question.

Your keeper question:

_____

_____

_____

_____

Write down some parts of the story that have something to do with your keeper question.

_____

_____

_____

_____

_____

_____

Into Reading
Determining Important Ideas

When you read, you decide which details are most important in helping you understand the story's main ideas or themes.

1. Find a place in the story you marked with a **!** and reread it. Write an important phrase or sentence from that part of the story.

_____

_____

_____

Now write what this phrase or sentence means, in your own words.

_____

_____

_____

Write the reasons why you think these words are important.

_____

_____

_____

Continue ⟶

2. Find a place in the story you marked with a ! and reread it. Write an important phrase or sentence from that part of the story.

_____

_____

Now write what this phrase or sentence means, in your own words.

_____

_____

Write the reasons why you think these words are important.

_____

_____

3. Find a place in the story you marked with a ! and reread it. Write an important phrase or sentence from that part of the story.

_____

_____

Now write what this phrase or sentence means, in your own words.

_____

_____

Write the reasons why you think these words are important.

_____

_____

Head in the Clouds

Use your imagination! Choose one of the topics in the clouds and draw a picture or write a little more about the story.

A part of
the story that
made me sad

A picture
of the
ugly duckling

Something
the story
reminds me of

A note to the
other swans

Building Your Answer

The focus question:

_____

_____

_____

Your answer before the discussion:

_____

_____

_____

Your answer after the discussion (you may change or add to your first answer):

_____

_____

_____

An answer you heard in the discussion that was different from yours:

_____

_____

_____

Writing to Explain
Retelling the Story

Prewriting Notes

> The **sequence of events** is the order in which things happen in the story.

Complete the chart, starting with what happens **after** the duckling decides to leave the cat, hen, and old woman and "go out into the wide world" (page 99). Then, use your notes to retell that part of the story to a partner in your own words.

Sequence of events

1. _____

   _____

2. _____

   _____

3. _____

   _____

4. _____

   _____

5. _____

   _____

Writing to Explain
Retelling the Story

Setting	Characters' responses
1. _____ _____	1. _____ _____
2. _____ _____	2. _____ _____
3. _____ _____	3. _____ _____
4. _____ _____	4. _____ _____
5. _____ _____	5. _____ _____

Writing to Explain
Retelling the Story

Writing a Draft

Write what happens in "The Ugly Duckling" after the duckling decides to leave the cat and hen and go out into the world. Use your own words and put the story events in the correct order. Use your prewriting notes to help you.

"The Ugly Duckling" in My Own Words

After the ugly duckling decided to leave the cat and the hen, _____

_____

_____

_____

_____

_____

_____

_____

_____

_____

_____

_____

_____

Writing to Explain

Retelling the Story

Use this page if you need more room.

_____

_____

_____

_____

_____

_____

_____

_____

_____

_____

_____

_____

_____

_____

_____

Writing to Explore
Advice for the Ugly Duckling

Prewriting Notes

Pretend you are the ugly duckling, and choose a problem from the story that you would like to ask your partner about.

Your problem:

_____

_____

_____

To help you think more about the problem, answer the questions below as if you were the ugly duckling.

When and where did you have this problem?

_____

_____

Why did this problem happen? (If you are not sure, then guess.)

_____

_____

_____

What did you do when this problem happened?

_____

_____

_____

Writing a Draft

Write your letter to your partner in the space below, asking for advice about your problem. Use the answers you came up with to help you write.

Dear _____,

I need your advice! _____

_____

_____

_____

_____

_____

_____

_____

_____

What should I do?

Sincerely,

Ugly Duckling

Read your partner's letter. Then write a letter by yourself in the space below, giving your advice to the ugly duckling.

Dear Ugly Duckling,

I have some advice for you. _____

_____

_____

_____

_____

_____

_____

_____

_____

I hope this solves your problem

Your friend,

_____

White Wave

Chinese folktale as told by Diane Wolkstein

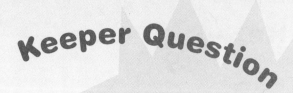

Keeper Question

In the space below, write down an interpretive question. Then write down two possible answers and a part of the story that supports each answer.

Your keeper question:

_____

_____

_____

_____

One way to answer the question: _____

_____

_____

A part of the story that shows this: _____

_____

_____

Another way to answer the question: _____

_____

_____

A part of the story that shows this: _____

_____

_____

Into Reading

Synthesizing

Synthesizing means you are thinking about different parts of a story and putting your thoughts together in a way that helps you understand the story's main ideas or themes. Synthesizing is like putting the pieces of a puzzle together to create a whole picture. When you synthesize, you use many other reading strategies, too.

In the box below, list in order three important events that happen after White Wave leaves Kuo Ming.

Important events (in order)

1. _____

_____

_____

_____

_____

2. _____

_____

_____

_____

3. _____

_____

_____

_____

Into Reading

Synthesizing

Look at the important events you listed on page 76. In the box below, write a summary about that part of the story.

Remember that a good **summary** includes enough information to explain what this part of the story is about, but not so much detail that you are just retelling the story. Your summary should be one to two sentences.

Summary

Now, in the box below, write your own thoughts about what happened in the story. You can write a question, a connection, an inference, your opinion, or anything else.

Your response

Head in the Clouds

Use your imagination! Choose one of the topics in the clouds and draw a picture or write a little more about the story.

A picture of White Wave

A picture of White Wave shrine

Someone I would build a shrine for, and why

How I felt at the end of the story

Building Your Answer

The focus question:

_____

_____

_____

Your answer before the discussion:

_____

_____

_____

Your answer after the discussion *(you may change or add to your first answer)*:

_____

_____

_____

Writing to Explain
Summarizing the Plot

Prewriting Notes

A story's **plot** is the sequence of events that occurs in the story. The plot also shows the characters' responses to those events.

Complete the plot chart below.

Sequence of events

1. _____

_____

2. _____

_____

3. _____

_____

4. _____

_____

5. _____

_____

Writing to Explain
Summarizing the Plot

Setting	Characters' responses
1. _____ _____	1. _____ _____
2. _____ _____	2. _____ _____
3. _____ _____	3. _____ _____
4. _____ _____	4. _____ _____
5. _____ _____	5. _____ _____

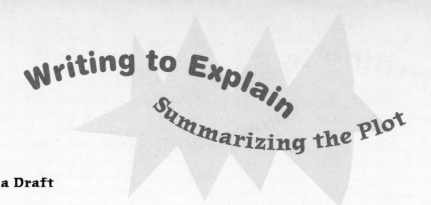

Writing to Explain
Summarizing the Plot

Writing a Draft

Now summarize "White Wave." Use your plot chart to help you remember important events in the story.

> To **summarize**, include enough information to explain what the story is about, but not so much detail that you are retelling the entire story step by step.

_____

_____

_____

_____

_____

_____

_____

_____

_____

_____

_____

_____

Writing to Explain
Summarizing the Plot

Use this space if you need more room.

_____

_____

_____

_____

_____

_____

_____

_____

_____

_____

_____

_____

_____

_____

_____

_____

_____

_____

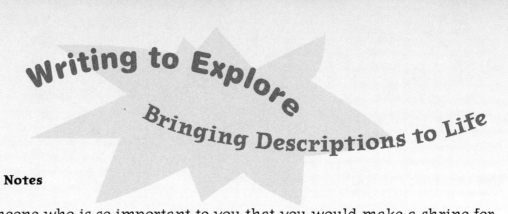

Writing to Explore
Bringing Descriptions to Life

Prewriting Notes

Choose someone who is so important to you that you would make a shrine for him or her, like Kuo Ming did for White Wave. Write down notes about this person and about the shrine you would build.

The person I would build a shrine for is _____ .

I would build it in honor of this person because _____

_____

_____

_____

_____

And also because _____

_____

_____

_____

_____

Here is what the shrine would look like: _____

_____

_____

_____

_____

_____

_____

_____

Writing to Explore
Bringing Descriptions to Life

Tell a partner why the person you chose is important to you and what the shrine would look like. Try to make each detail come alive with the way you use your voice.

Write down some more details you thought of while working with your partner.

More about the person and why I chose him or her: _____

_____

_____

_____

_____

More about the shrine: _____

_____

_____

_____

Writing a Draft

Write your description of the person who is important to you and the shrine you would build for that person. Think about how you described the person and the shrine to your partner and use your prewriting notes on pages 84–86 to help you.

_____

_____

_____

_____

_____

_____

_____

_____

_____

_____

_____

_____

_____

Writing to Explore
Bringing Descriptions to Life

Now draw a picture of your shrine.

The Mousewife

Rumer Godden

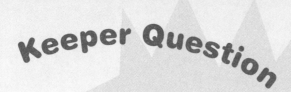

Keeper Question

In the space below, write down an interpretive question. Then write down two possible answers and a part of the story that supports each answer.

Your keeper question:

_____

_____

_____

_____

One way to answer the question: _____

_____

_____

A part of the story that shows this: _____

_____

_____

Another way to answer the question: _____

_____

_____

A part of the story that shows this: _____

_____

_____

Synthesizing means you are thinking about different parts of a story and putting your thoughts together in a way that helps you understand the story's main ideas or themes. Synthesizing is like putting the pieces of a puzzle together to create a whole picture. When you synthesize, you use many other reading strategies, too.

In the box below, list in order three important events that happen after the mousewife goes to see the dove for the last time (page 132).

Important events (in order)

1. _____
   _____
   _____
   _____

2. _____
   _____
   _____
   _____

3. _____
   _____
   _____
   _____

Into Reading

Synthesizing

Look at the important events you listed on page 91. In the box below, write a summary about that part of the story.

> Remember that a good **summary** includes enough information to explain what this part of the story is about, but not so much detail that you are just retelling the story step by step. Your summary should be one to two sentences.

Summary

Now, in the box below, write your own thoughts about what happened in the story. You can write a question, a connection, an inference, your opinion, or anything else.

Your response

Head in the Clouds

Use your imagination! Choose one of the topics in the clouds and draw a picture or write a little more about the story.

A picture of the dove escaping

Something the story makes me think of

A note from the mousewife to her husband

How I felt at the end of the story

Building Your Answer

The focus question:

_____

_____

_____

Your answer before the discussion:

_____

_____

_____

Your answer after the discussion (you may change or add to your first answer):

_____

_____

_____

Two quotes or brief passages from the story that support your answer:

1. _____

_____

_____

2. _____

_____

_____

Prewriting Notes

Choose a theme. Then complete the web below by filling in evidence from the story that supports that theme.

A **theme** is a major idea in a story. A theme goes beyond the characters and events in the story. It has to do with the story's overall meaning or with something important the author is trying to say.

Theme:

_____

_____

_____

_____

Writing to Explain
Writing About Theme

Evidence: (page _____)

_____

_____

_____

_____

_____

Evidence: (page _____)

_____

_____

_____

_____

_____

Evidence: (page _____)

_____

_____

_____

_____

_____

Writing to Explain
Writing About Theme

Writing a Draft

Write an essay explaining the theme you chose and giving evidence from the story that tells the reader about that theme.

_____

_____

_____

_____

_____

_____

_____

_____

_____

_____

_____

_____

_____

_____

_____

_____

_____

Writing to Explain
Writing About Theme

Use this page if you need more room.

_____

_____

_____

_____

_____

_____

_____

_____

_____

_____

_____

_____

_____

_____

_____

_____

Writing to Explore
Wish You Were Here

Prewriting Notes

Think of a place that the dove might visit and write it down in the center of the web. In the other boxes, write details about the place and about how the dove might feel in this place.

Detail:

_____

_____

_____

Detail:

_____

_____

Place:

_____

Detail:

_____

_____

_____

Detail:

_____

_____

_____

Writing a Draft

Select a few of your favorite details from your prewriting notes to write a postcard from the dove to the mousewife after the dove escapes from his cage. The postcard should be about a place he might visit and about how he might feel being in that place.

A Postcard from the Dove

Dear Mousewife,

_____

_____

_____

_____

_____

_____

_____

The Mousewife
Miss Wilkinson's House

Your friend,
The Dove

Now complete the front of your postcard. Draw a picture of the setting you described on the other side of your postcard.

How the Tortoise Became

Ted Hughes

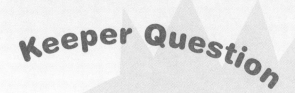

Keeper Question

In the space below, write down an interpretive question. Then write down two possible answers and a passage from the story that supports each answer.

Your keeper question:

_____

_____

_____

One way to answer the question: _____

_____

_____

A passage that supports this answer: _____

_____

_____ (page _____)

Another way to answer the question: _____

_____

_____

A passage that supports this answer: _____

_____

_____ (page _____)

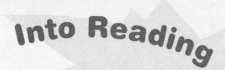

Into Reading

Synthesizing

Synthesizing means you are thinking about different parts of a story and putting your thoughts together in a way that helps you understand the story's main ideas or themes. Synthesizing is like putting the pieces of a puzzle together to create a whole picture. When you synthesize, you use many other reading strategies, too.

In the box below, list in order three important events that happen after Torto finally accepts a skin from God.

Important events (in order)

1. _____

   _____

   _____

   _____

2. _____

   _____

   _____

   _____

3. _____

   _____

   _____

   _____

Into Reading

Synthesizing

Look at the important events you listed on page 106. In the box below, write a summary about that part of the story.

> **Summary**
>
> _____
>
> _____
>
> _____
>
> _____

In the box below, write your own thoughts about what happened in the story. You can write a question, a connection, an inference, your opinion, or anything else.

> **Your response**
>
> _____
>
> _____
>
> _____
>
> _____

Continue ⟶

Into Reading

Synthesizing

Now, in the box below, write a main idea you see in this part of the story. What message might readers take away from the story? What might the author be trying to tell us?

A main idea

Head in the Clouds

Use your imagination! Choose one of the topics in the clouds and draw a picture or write a little more about the story.

A part of the story that I thought was funny

A picture of the race at the end of the story

Something in the story am still wondering about

Why I like the skin that I have

Building Your Answer

The focus question:

_____

_____

_____

Your answer before the discussion:

_____

_____

_____

Your answer after the discussion _(you may change or add to your first answer)_:

_____

_____

_____

Another answer you heard in the discussion that is different from yours:

_____

_____

_____

Writing to Explain
Writing About Theme

Prewriting Notes

Write one of the story's themes in the large box below. Then on page 113, write evidence from the story that supports this theme.

Explain your theme and the evidence to a partner. If your partner does not understand something, decide together what you can add or how you can make it clearer.

Finally, complete the web by explaining how your evidence supports the theme you chose.

> A **theme** is a major idea in a story. A theme goes beyond the characters and events in the story. It has to do with the story's meaning or with something important the author is trying to say.

Theme:

_____

_____

_____

_____

Writing to Explain
Writing About Theme

Evidence: (page _____)

_____

_____

_____

_____

Explanation:

_____

_____

_____

_____

_____

Evidence: (page _____)

_____

_____

_____

_____

Explanation:

_____

_____

_____

_____

_____

Evidence: (page _____)

_____

_____

_____

_____

Explanation:

_____

_____

_____

_____

_____

Writing to Explain
Writing About Theme

Writing a Draft

Write an essay about the theme you see in the story. Convince your readers by using evidence from the story and explaining how your evidence supports the theme.

_____

_____

_____

_____

_____

_____

_____

_____

_____

_____

_____

_____

_____

_____

_____

_____

Writing to Explain
Writing About Theme

Use this page if you need more room.

_____

_____

_____

_____

_____

_____

_____

_____

_____

_____

_____

_____

_____

_____

_____

_____

Writing to Explore
A Folktale

Prewriting Notes

The animal I have chosen for my folktale is _____.

> **These questions might help you think of important features:**
>
> | | |
> | --- | --- |
> | What does your animal look like? | What does it sound like? |
> | How does it act? | What does it eat? |
> | Where can it be found? | Who are its friends? Enemies? |

Now write down some important features about your animal.

_____

_____

_____

_____

_____

Circle the feature you would like to write your **why** or **how** question about. This is the question you will answer in your folktale.

Now write your **why** or **how** question.

_____

_____

On the next page, make some notes about the beginning, middle, and end of your tale.

Writing to Explore
A Folktale

Your tale's **beginning** (describes how the animal used to be)

Example: Torto is the fastest runner because he has no skin.

_____

_____

_____

Your tale's **middle** (tells about a problem or a change and what happened because of it)

Example: Torto asks for a skin he can take off and put on whenever he wants.

_____

_____

_____

Your tale's **end** (describes how the animal is now because of what happened)

Example: Torto's shell slows him down. The animals say, "Who's the slowest? Torto is." So now he is called Tortoise.

_____

_____

_____

Writing to Explore
A Folktale

Writing a Draft

Using your notes, write your folktale in the space below.

_____

In the beginning, _____

_____

_____

_____

_____

_____

Then one day, _____

_____

_____

_____

_____

_____

_____

Continue ⟶

Writing to Explore

A Folktale

So from that time on, _____

_____

_____

_____

_____

_____

Use the rest of the page if you need more room.

_____

_____

_____

_____

_____

_____

_____

_____

_____

_____

_____

Two Wise Children

Robert Graves

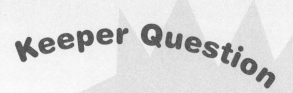

Keeper Question

In the space below, write down an interpretive question. Then write down two possible answers and a passage from the story that supports each answer.

Your keeper question:

_____

_____

_____

One way to answer the question: _____

_____

_____

A passage that supports this answer: _____

_____

_____ (page _____)

Another way to answer the question: _____

_____

_____

A passage that supports this answer: _____

_____

_____ (page _____)

Into Reading

Synthesizing

Synthesizing means you are thinking about different parts of a story and putting your thoughts together in a way that helps you understand the story's main ideas or themes. Synthesizing is like putting the pieces of a puzzle together to create a whole picture. When you synthesize, you use many other reading strategies, too.

In the box below, list in order three important events that happen after Bill decides to fight the bull.

Important events (in order)

1. _____

2. _____

3. _____

Into Reading

Synthesizing

Look at the important events you listed on page 124. In the box below, write a summary about that part of the story.

Summary

_____

_____

_____

In the box below, write your own thoughts about what happened in the story. You can write a question, a connection, an inference, your opinion, or anything else.

Your response

_____

_____

_____

_____

Continue ⟶

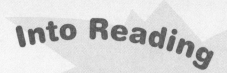

Now, in the box below, write a main idea you see in this part of the story. What message might readers take away from the story? What might the author be trying to tell us?

A main idea

Head in the Clouds

Use your imagination! Choose one of the topics in the clouds and draw a picture or write a little more about the story.

A picture of Avis's needlework

My favorite character in the story

Something in the story that I am curious about

A magic power would like to have, and why

Building Your Answer

The focus question:

_____

_____

_____

Your answer before the discussion:

_____

_____

_____

Your answer after the discussion (you may change or add to your first answer):

_____

_____

_____

To support your answer, write one piece of evidence from the story **or** something you heard in the discussion (circle one):

_____

_____

_____

_____

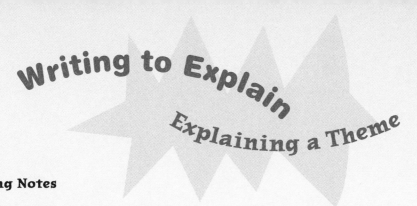

Writing to Explain
Explaining a Theme

Prewriting Notes

Many parts, or **elements**, make up a great story. You have learned about a number of story elements: character, plot, setting, and language (such as imagery and similes). You have also learned about theme. Writing about the other story elements can help you explain a theme you see in the story.

Write a theme you see in the story:

_____

_____

_____

Circle one or two other story elements you will write about to help you explain the theme you chose.

Character   **Language**   **Plot**   **Setting**

Continue   ⟶

Writing to Explain
Explaining a Theme

Story element 1: _____

How it helps you explain the theme:

_____

_____

_____

_____

_____

Story element 2: _____

How it helps you explain the theme:

_____

_____

_____

_____

_____

Writing to Explain
Explaining a Theme

Writing a Draft

Write about a theme you see in the story "Two Wise Children." Show how other story elements help you explain this theme. Remember to use evidence from the story.

_____

_____

_____

_____

_____

_____

_____

_____

_____

_____

_____

_____

_____

Writing to Explain
Explaining a Theme

Use this page if you need more room.

_____

_____

_____

_____

_____

_____

_____

_____

_____

_____

_____

_____

_____

_____

_____

_____

_____

_____

_____

_____

Writing to Explore
A Secret Power

Prewriting Notes

If I could have a secret power, it would be _____

_____

_____

I would want this power because _____

_____

_____

_____

On the next page, take some notes about the beginning, middle, and end of your story.

Writing to Explore
A Secret Power

Your story's **beginning** (a description of the power you have and why you have it)

_____

_____

_____

_____

Your story's **middle** (the problem or change—how your power was discovered)

_____

_____

_____

_____

Your story's **end** (what happened after your power was discovered, and how you felt because of what happened)

_____

_____

_____

_____

Writing to Explore

A Secret Power

Writing a Draft

Using your notes, write your story in the space below.

MY SECRET POWER— DISCOVERED!

_____

_____

_____

_____

_____

_____

_____

_____

_____

_____

_____

_____

_____

Writing to Explore
A Secret Power

Use this page if you need more room.

_____

_____

_____

_____

_____

_____

_____

_____

_____

_____

_____

_____

_____

_____

_____

_____

_____

_____

_____

Writing Notebook

This is your chance to look back at what you have written in your Reader's Journal, choose a piece you wrote that you like, and make it the best it can be. Here's how to revise your draft:

1. Choose a Writing to Explain piece you wrote that you would most like to revise.

2. Mark the page with a paper clip or a sticky note and turn in your Reader's Journal to your teacher. Your teacher will write a question or note on pages 140, 144, or 148 for you to think about.

3. Read and think about your teacher's note. Review the story and your Reader's Journal for more ideas.

4. Plan your revised writing in the prewriting notes section on pages 141, 145, or 149. Then write your revised draft on the page after.

Writing Notebook
Planning Page

Choose a piece to revise about one of these stories (circle one):

The Dream Weaver   **Jean Labadie's Big Black Dog**   **Caporushes**

It is on page _____ of the Reader's Journal.

Think about your teacher's note to help you make your writing shine.

_____ **Write more details about character traits.**

Teacher's note: _____

_____

_____

_____

_____ **Explain the problems and solutions more clearly.**

Teacher's note: _____

_____

_____

_____

_____ **Add or change words to make a simile clearer.**

Teacher's note: _____

_____

_____

_____

Writing Notebook
Planning Page

Prewriting Notes

Use a web, a chart, or a list to plan your writing.

Writing Notebook
Final Draft

_____

_____

_____

_____

_____

_____

_____

_____

_____

_____

_____

_____

_____

_____

_____

_____

_____

_____

Writing Notebook
Final Draft

Use this page if you need more room.

_____

_____

_____

_____

_____

_____

_____

_____

_____

_____

_____

_____

_____

_____

_____

_____

_____

Writing Notebook
Planning Page

Choose a piece to revise about one of these stories (circle one):

The Upside-Down Boy   **The Green Man**   **The Ugly Duckling**

It is on page _____ of the Reader's Journal.

Think about your teacher's note to help you make your writing shine.

_____ **Give more evidence to support your main idea.**

Teacher's note: _____

_____

_____

_____

_____ **Write a litle more about imagery or setting.**

Teacher's note: _____

_____

_____

_____

_____ **Retell the important events in the story in order, using your own words.**

Teacher's note: _____

_____

_____

_____

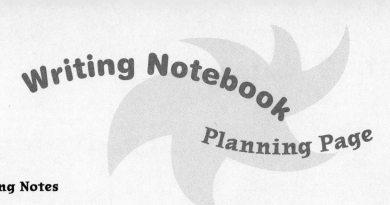

Writing Notebook
Planning Page

Prewriting Notes

Use a web, a chart, or a list to plan your writing.

Writing Notebook

Final Draft

_____

_____
_____
_____
_____
_____
_____
_____
_____
_____
_____
_____
_____
_____
_____
_____
_____
_____
_____

Writing Notebook
Final Draft

Use this page if you need more room.

_____

_____

_____

_____

_____

_____

_____

_____

_____

_____

_____

_____

_____

_____

_____

_____

_____

Writing Notebook
Planning Page

Choose a piece to revise about one of these stories (circle one):

White Wave   **The Mousewife**

How the Tortoise Became   **Two Wise Children**

It is on page _____ of the Reader's Journal.

Think about your teacher's note to help you make your writing shine.

_____ **Include important events in your story summary without going into too much detail.**

Teacher's note: _____

_____

_____

_____ **Explain more about a theme in the story.**

Teacher's note: _____

_____

_____

_____ **Write more about a story element such as setting, plot, or character in the story.**

Teacher's note: _____

_____

_____

Writing Notebook

Planning Page

Prewriting Notes

Use a web, a chart, or a list to plan your writing.

Writing Notebook
Final Draft

_____

_____

_____

_____

_____

_____

_____

_____

_____

_____

_____

_____

_____

_____

_____

_____

_____

_____

_____

_____

Writing Notebook
Final Draft

Use this page if you need more room.

_____

_____

_____

_____

_____

_____

_____

_____

_____

_____

_____

_____

_____

_____

_____

_____

_____

_____

Curious Words

For each story, write down a curious word and the page number where the word appears. Then do one of the following:

• Write why you like your curious word, why it seems curious to you, or why you remember it.

• Pretend that one of the characters in the story uses your curious word and write down something the character says.

• Use your curious word in a message—for example, in a birthday card, in a poem, or in a funny note to a friend.

• Make up a fun way to use the word yourself.

Curious Words

The Dream Weaver

Your curious word _____ **page** _____

_____

_____

_____

Your curious word _____ **page** _____

_____

_____

_____

Your curious word _____ **page** _____

_____

_____

_____

Curious Words

Jean Labadie's Big Black Dog

Your curious word _____ **page** _____

_____

_____

_____

Your curious word _____ **page** _____

_____

_____

_____

Your curious word _____ **page** _____

_____

_____

_____

Curious Words

Caporushes

Your curious word _____ **page** _____

_____

_____

_____

Your curious word _____ **page** _____

_____

_____

_____

Your curious word _____ **page** _____

_____

_____

_____

Curious Words

The Upside-Down Boy

Your curious word _____ **page** _____

_____

_____

_____

Your curious word _____ **page** _____

_____

_____

_____

Your curious word _____ **page** _____

_____

_____

_____

Curious Words

The Green Man

Your curious word _____ **page** _____

_____

_____

_____

Your curious word _____ **page** _____

_____

_____

_____

Your curious word _____ **page** _____

_____

_____

_____

Curious Words

The Ugly Duckling

Your curious word _____ page _____

_____

_____

_____

Your curious word _____ page _____

_____

_____

_____

Your curious word _____ page _____

_____

_____

_____

Curious Words

White Wave

Your curious word _____ **page** _____

_____

_____

_____

Your curious word _____ **page** _____

_____

_____

_____

Your curious word _____ **page** _____

_____

_____

_____

Curious Words

The Mousewife

Your curious word _____ **page** _____

_____

_____

_____

Your curious word _____ **page** _____

_____

_____

_____

Your curious word _____ **page** _____

_____

_____

_____

Curious Words

How the Tortoise Became

Your curious word _____ **page** _____

_____

_____

_____

Your curious word _____ **page** _____

_____

_____

_____

Your curious word _____ **page** _____

_____

_____

_____

Curious Words

Two Wise Children

Your curious word _____ **page** _____

_____

_____

_____

Your curious word _____ **page** _____

_____

_____

_____

Your curious word _____ **page** _____

_____

_____

_____

Glossary

In this glossary, you'll find definitions for words that you may not know, but that are in the stories you've read. You'll find the meaning of each word as it is used in the story. The word may have other meanings as well, which you can find in a dictionary if you're interested. If you don't find a word here that you're wondering about, go to your dictionary for help.

accord: When things happen of their own **accord**, they happen without being forced. Your heart beats of its own **accord**—you don't have to make it beat. If you cleaned your room before your mother told you to, you'd be doing it of your own **accord**.

accustomed: If you are **accustomed** to something, you are used to it. If you go to bed every night at nine o'clock, you will become **accustomed** to going to sleep at that time.

admires: To **admire** something is to look at it with pleasure and to like it. My parents stopped to **admire** the beautiful sunset. My best friend always **admires** the cakes in the bakery window.

adversity: Great difficulty or suffering. Someone who survived a bad accident might say they made it through much **adversity**. It is often said that we become stronger when we face **adversity**.

agile: You are **agile** if you are able to move quickly and easily. Someone who does gymnastics or plays basketball must be **agile**. The **agile** monkey swung from tree to tree with great speed.

agog: Somebody **agog** is very excited about something. You might be **agog** when your teacher announces that you will be going on a mystery field trip.

agony: A feeling of great pain or suffering. The soccer player cried out in **agony** when he broke his arm.

amuse: If you **amuse** someone, you make that person laugh or smile by doing something funny or pleasing. You might **amuse** your little sister by making funny faces at her.

appallingly: Something **appalling** fills you with a feeling of shock along with fear or dislike. My room was so **appallingly** dirty, I couldn't invite anyone over, and it took the whole day to clean it up.

aristocratic: Someone who is **aristocratic** is thought to be very important because of family background. The children of a queen and king are thought to be **aristocratic**.

arrogant: An **arrogant** person thinks he or she is better than other people and often acts rude or snobby. There is an **arrogant** girl in my class who never listens to the teacher and thinks she is smarter than the other students. If you behave in an **arrogant** way, people might think you are stuck-up.

astonished: You are **astonished** when you are surprised or shocked by something because it is so unusual or unexpected. You might be **astonished** if your mother served you ice cream for breakfast or your cat walked on its hind legs.

au revoir: French for *goodbye*.

balconies: A **balcony** is a platform that sticks out from the outside wall of a building with railings around it for safety. Houses and apartment buildings sometimes have **balconies** where people can sit and enjoy the fresh air.

beaters: In a hunt, a **beater** is a person who hits the bushes so that the animals or birds will come out into the open. Once the **beaters** have scared the ducks from their hiding places, it is easier for the hunters to aim at them.

bestowed: To **bestow on** or **bestow upon** means to give something, usually a gift or a prize. Your teacher might **bestow** gifts on the class for good attendance.

blacksmith: A **blacksmith** is a person who makes horseshoes and other things out of iron. The **blacksmith** shapes the iron by heating it over a fire and then hammering it while it is still hot.

boasting: To **boast** is to talk about yourself with too much pride. I wish you would stop **boasting** about your wonderful grades all the time.

bobbin: A spool that holds thread or yarn for weaving or sewing.

brim: The top edge of a container. Her glass was filled to the **brim** with water, so she carried it very carefully to the table.

briskly: When you do something **briskly,** you do it quickly and with much energy. You might walk **briskly** to the bus stop if you were late for school.

broach: If you **broach** an idea or a subject as you speak to someone, you bring it up because you want to talk about it. You might not want to **broach** the subject of going to the playground with your parents if they are tired. If your friend said something mean behind your back, you might **broach** the problem by asking him if he is angry with you for something.

brooch: A **brooch** is a large, fancy pin. Most **brooches** are made of silver, gold, or other jewels, and you wear them pinned on your clothes. The word **brooch** is pronounced the same way as *broach* (see above), but they have different meanings.

brooding: Sitting on eggs until they hatch. Farmers often build henhouses so that hens have a safe place for **brooding**.

brooded: To **brood** is to worry or think very seriously about something for a long time. I **brooded** over a fight I had with a friend.

buenos días: Spanish for *good morning* or *good day*.

buffeted: To **buffet** something is to hit or shake it roughly. The giant ocean waves **buffeted** the small boat so much that it almost sank.

butt: A person or thing that is made fun of. If you wore a silly costume to school and it wasn't Halloween, you might be the **butt** of everyone's jokes.

calling: Your **calling** is the work you feel you are meant to do in life. I am good at math, but writing poetry is my true **calling**.

campesinos: Spanish for *people who live in the country*.

campo: Spanish for *countryside*.

capable: If you are **capable**, you are able to do many things well. We were not sure he could handle so many difficult tasks, but it turned out that he was a **capable** person. If you are a **capable** student, you might want to sign up for the spelling bee and the science fair.

caressed: To **caress** something means to touch or stroke it gently. My sister **caressed** the horse's silky nose.

cascaded: To **cascade** is to fall or flow down in a way that looks like a waterfall. The beads from the broken necklace **cascaded** to the floor.

castanets: Small shell-shaped musical instruments, usually made of wood, that you wear on your fingers. You click **castanets** together to the beat of a song.

chico: Spanish for *boy*.

chided: To **chide** is to speak in a way that shows you are disappointed in someone. The teacher **chided** me for forgetting my homework.

choir: A **choir** is a group of singers. The church has a **choir** that sings during the services.

cinnamon: A reddish-brown spice. People bake **cinnamon** in muffins and cakes, and put it in oatmeal.

collided: When people or things **collide**, they bump or crash into each other. The two cars were dented badly when they **collided**.

companion: Someone who spends time with you; a friend. Your **companions** are the people you do things with.

conceited: You are **conceited** if you are too proud of yourself and the things you can do. Nobody in the class would talk to the **conceited** student who always talked about the time he had a part on a television show.

consequently: As a result. I jumped in a puddle; **consequently**, my shoes got soaking wet.

console: To comfort or cheer up a person. Your mother might try to **console** you if you were sick and had to miss the class field trip to the zoo.

counsel: Advice or a plan about what to do. When you keep your own **counsel**, you follow your own plans or ideas.

cowered: When you **cower**, you curl up to make yourself smaller, usually because you are afraid or are trying to protect yourself. When the barking dog ran toward me, I **cowered** in the corner.

craned: When you **crane,** you stretch your neck to try and see something better. I was sitting in the back of the class, so I **craned** my neck to see the board.

cumber, cumbered: Something might **cumber** you if it gets in your way or weighs you down. A heavy backpack might **cumber** you if you are trying to run to the bus stop. She tried to walk quickly, but she was **cumbered** by her long skirt.

currants: Small, seedless raisins often used in baking.

daze: If you are in a **daze**, you are not thinking or speaking very clearly. I was in such a **daze** after I got hit with the ball that I could only stare into space.

defiantly: When you do something **defiantly**, you boldly stand up to something or someone; you refuse to follow orders. The student **defiantly** refused to line up with the other children.

delicate: Something that is **delicate** is dainty, finely detailed and pleasing to look at. The lace on my handmade shawl is very **delicate**.

delighted: If you are **delighted**, you are very pleased. You might be **delighted** to go to a friend's birthday party.

dense: Very thick or crowded together. The forest was so **dense** that hardly any sunlight reached the ground. The **densest** fog is impossible to see through.

despised: A person or thing that is **despised** is disliked very much. The ugly school colors were **despised** by everyone, so we voted to change them.

disadvantage: A **disadvantage** is something that causes problems or makes it hard to be successful. If you are at a pool or beach and don't know how to swim, you are at a **disadvantage**. It is a **disadvantage** to be without an eraser if you make a lot of mistakes on your math homework.

disgraced: You are **disgraced** if you do something that causes people to look down on you or lose respect for you. The students were **disgraced** when the teacher caught them cheating on a test. He was **disgraced** at the game by fighting with a player on the other team.

disgusted: If you are **disgusted** by something, it causes you feelings of strong dislike or makes you feel sick to your stomach. You might be **disgusted** if you accidentally got chewing gum all over your new sneakers.

dismay: A loss of courage, often in the face of danger or difficulty. The hikers were in **dismay** to find the mountain trail erased by the rain.

distaffs: A **distaff** is a stick that holds wool ready to be pulled off little by little to make into yarn or thread. **Distaffs** are often attached to spinning wheels.

distinction: A **distinction** is something that makes a person or a thing special, excellent, or unusual. It is a great **distinction** to receive first prize in a writing contest.

downhearted: If you are **downhearted**, you feel sad or gloomy. You might be **downhearted** if your best friend moved away. A cold, rainy day always makes me feel a little **downhearted**.

downright: Completely or totally. We were **downright** tired after spending all day at the beach.

drake: A male duck.

eager: You are **eager** if you are very interested in and excited about something. You might be **eager** to go to the store if they have a new game that you really want to buy. I was not **eager** to go outside because it was pouring rain.

earthenware: A type of clay pottery. **Earthenware** is baked in a *kiln* (a pottery oven) at a low temperature.

elegant: Describes something that is stylish and in good taste. The palace was filled with **elegant** furniture covered in beautiful fabrics. We celebrated my grandmother's birthday with an **elegant** candlelit dinner.

enthusiastically: When you do something **enthusiastically**, you do it with great excitement, interest, and energy. My friend had been waiting for me to arrive and greeted me **enthusiastically.**

envy: When you **envy** someone, you feel uncomfortable because you wish you could have something that person has. I do not **envy** my friend for his new lunch box, because I like to carry my lunch in a paper bag.

exceedingly: Very, very much; more than is usual. The man who owns that big house is **exceedingly** rich. Even though it was the first day of winter, it was **exceedingly** warm.

exclaimed: You **exclaim** when you speak suddenly because you are surprised or excited. My mother **exclaimed**, "I'm so proud of you!" when I set the table all by myself.

fen: A low, wet area of land. Frogs, mosquitoes, and water bugs might live in a **fen**.

fender: A **fender** is a metal screen placed in front of a fireplace to keep sparks from flying into the room.

fierce: Wild, mean, and dangerous. You should never get close to **fierce** animals or they may bite, scratch, or kick you.

fiesta: Spanish for *party*.

flourished: To **flourish** is to grow well and become strong. Plants will **flourish** if you give them the sunlight and water they need. The shopkeeper's business **flourished** once he started advertising in the newspaper.

flushed: If you are **flushed**, you have turned red, often from hard exercise or embarrassment. Your face may be **flushed** after you run all the way around the gym.

foreboding: A feeling that something bad is about to happen. If you are at a very scary movie, you might watch the screen with **foreboding**. She had a sense of **foreboding** when she heard her friend start to cry in the next room.

frantic: If you are **frantic**, you are very excited by worry and fear. You might be **frantic** if you thought you lost your brand-new coat.

frisked: To **frisk** is to move around playfully and quickly. The hamster **frisked** around the room, playing with a piece of string.

frolic: A **frolic** is happy, carefree play. You might have a **frolic** in the snow with your friends at recess.

gallery: In a theater, castle, or large house, the **gallery** is an upstairs sitting or standing area that looks down on a large room. Many guests at the party were up in the **gallery**, watching the dancers in the ballroom below.

gazing: To **gaze** is to stare or to look at something steadily and for a long time. She spent a long time **gazing** into the mirror at her new haircut.

generous: If you give your friend a **generous** amount of your candy, you give him a large portion. My mother gave me a **generous** piece of apple pie because she knows it is my favorite kind.

gilt: Describes something covered with a thin layer of gold or gold-colored paint. Paintings in museums often have **gilt** frames around them.

gleaner: Someone who picks up the grain left behind in a field after crops have been gathered.

glided: To **glide** is to move smoothly and easily, without any effort. The skater **glided** on the ice without falling down once.

glistening: Shining or sparkling in the light. The snow was **glistening** in the bright sunlight.

glorious: Beautiful and wonderful. It was a **glorious** spring day, so we played outside all afternoon long.

grope: To **grope** is to feel around with your hands for something. If I **grope** under the couch, maybe I will find the marble that rolled there.

gruel: A very thin porridge or soup.

hamlet: A small village.

handiwork: Your **handiwork** is anything you have made yourself, by hand. Knitting and making clay pots are two examples of **handiwork**.

harmonica: A **harmonica** is a small rectangular musical instrument with slots that you blow in and out of.

hawking: Using trained hawks for hunting.

hillock: A small hill.

hospitable: To be **hospitable** is to treat visitors or guests in a friendly and welcoming way. You would be **hospitable** if you invited your new neighbors over for dinner. The server at our favorite restaurant is very **hospitable** and always greets us with a big smile.

idling: If you are **idling**, you are not doing any work. The children spent their time **idling** in front of the TV instead of doing their homework.

ignorant: To be **ignorant** is to have very little knowledge or education about something. If you visited another country, you might be **ignorant** about the customs there. He said some **ignorant** things in class because he had not read the book.

implored: To **implore** is to beg or ask for something very seriously. You might **implore** your parents for a later bedtime. The prisoner **implored** the judge to let him go free.

inattentive: If you are being **inattentive,** you are not paying attention. You might be **inattentive** in math class if you already knew how to do the problems.

incompetent: Someone **incompetent** doesn't know how to do something or is not able to do something well. You might be **incompetent** at playing the piano if you never took lessons or practiced.

indecent: Something **indecent** is rude or shocking. It was **indecent** of our guest to get up and leave right in the middle of dinner.

indigestion: When you eat something that is hard for your body to break down (digest), you might get **indigestion**, which is a painful or uncomfortable feeling in your stomach. Spicy foods give some people **indigestion**.

intently: When people do things **intently**, they focus on what they're doing and give it all their attention. Basketball players need to look at the basket **intently** when they try to make a free throw.

jabbering: To **jabber** is to talk very fast or in a way that is hard to understand. Babies might start **jabbering** before they learn to say real words.

jeering: To **jeer** is to make fun of someone or say mean things to someone in a rude way. The mean older boys are always **jeering** at us from across the street when we walk to school. Nobody could hear the man give his speech because the crowd was **jeering** so loudly.

jersey: A **jersey** is a pullover sweater or shirt made of soft, knitted fabric.

just: Fair and right. A judge tries to make a **just** decision after hearing both sides of a story in court.

kernels: Grains or seeds of corn, wheat, or other plants. The single pieces of corn in corn on the cob are the **kernels**.

larders: A **larder** is a room or closet where food is stored.

lavish: Describes something when it is more than is needed or grand and expensive. My great-uncle is known for throwing **lavish** parties with fancy food and decorations.

leaner: Thinner or with less fat. People who get lots of exercise are often **leaner** than people who don't.

lichen: A life form that can sometimes look like moss or thin ropes.

linen: A kind of cloth made from a plant called *flax*. **Linen** is often used to make clothing, tablecloths, napkins, and sheets.

linnets: A **linnet** is a small brown bird. **Linnets** are found in Europe, Asia, and Africa.

lodged: To be **lodged** is to be stuck or to stay in place. The kite was **lodged** in the tree and wouldn't come down, no matter how hard we pulled its string.

longing: To have a **longing** is to want or wish for something very much. If you are very thirsty, you might have a **longing** for a huge glass of lemonade. All her life, the woman has had a **longing** to visit a far-away country.

looms: A **loom** is a machine or frame used to weave thread or yarn into cloth.

lumbered: To **lumber** is to move in a slow, clumsy way. My father **lumbered** up the stairs, carrying two heavy suitcases at the same time.

manufacture: To **manufacture** something is to make it, usually with a machine. The factory down the street **manufactures** cars.

marsh: A low, soft, wet area of land.

marvelous: Something that is **marvelous** causes wonder or amazement. There might be a **marvelous** fireworks display on the Fourth of July. Something **marvelous** can also be excellent. We cooked with **marvelous** food fresh from the garden.

mayhap: An old-fashioned way of saying *maybe* or *perhaps*.

meandering: Something that is **meandering** is following a twisting and turning path. A river **meandering** through a valley might look like a long, winding snake if you saw it from above.

measure: While it means many other things as well, a **measure** can be a kind of dance.

medal: A **medal** is a piece of metal, usually flat and round, that is given to a person as a prize for winning, being brave, or doing something very important. You might get a **medal** for winning a race.

milestones: A **milestone** is a stone marker found at the side of a road that tells the distance to another place.

mindful: To be **mindful** is to be aware of or to pay careful attention to something. If you have to be home by six o'clock, you should be **mindful** of the time when you are out playing. When I put away the dishes after dinner, I try to be **mindful** of how easily they can break.

miserable: Very unhappy or uncomfortable. Having a bad cold can make you feel **miserable**.

mite: A **mite** is a very tiny amount. I cleaned the kitchen floor so well that there wasn't a **mite** of dirt on it.

moat: Long ago, people might dig a **moat**—a long, deep ditch all the way around a castle or a town—to protect it from enemies. A **moat** is usually filled with water, and people must use a bridge to cross it.

mortar: A deep, strong bowl in which grains, herbs, or nuts can be crushed with a tool called a *pestle*.

nimble: To be **nimble** is to move quickly and lightly. A tightrope walker at the circus has to be **nimble** to stay balanced high up in the air.

noble: To be **noble** is to be grand and glorious in appearance. The American eagle is a **noble** bird.

nuzzled: To **nuzzle** is to rub or touch something gently with the nose. My dog **nuzzled** my hand happily when I got home from school.

obliged: If you are **obliged** to do something, you have to do it—you have no choice. If you were to spill your friend's milk, you might feel **obliged** to give her some of yours.

occupation: Your **occupation** is the job you do to earn a living. Being a doctor is a fine **occupation** because you can help people get well. His grandmother's **occupation** was teaching school, but her hobby was doing crossword puzzles.

oilcloth: A piece of cloth that has been covered in oil, clay, or special paint to make it waterproof.

pandemonium: Noisy confusion. There would be **pandemonium** at a circus if the tent were to cave in.

parish: A **parish** is an area that has its own church and its own priest or minister.

pat: A **pat** answer is one that fits the question, but might be too quick or perfect. Whenever someone asks me, "How are you?" my **pat** answer is "Fine."

peasants: In earlier times, a person who worked on a farm was called a **peasant**. There were many **peasants** in Europe and parts of Asia.

peering: To **peer** is to look at something very closely and with interest. You might **peer** at someone you think you know from school, but aren't quite sure. To **peer** also means to look hard at something that is difficult to see. My sister was **peering** into the dark closet to see if her sneakers were in there.

perched: To **perch** is to sit, stand, or rest on something that is raised. I **perched** on a tall stool so that I could see out the window.

persecuted: If you are **persecuted**, you are treated very badly, over and over. I was **persecuted** by the neighborhood bully, who called me names every time I walked by her. The man was so **persecuted** by his nasty neighbors that he decided to move to another part of town.

pestle: A **pestle** is a small tool with a round end used to crush or grind things in a deep bowl called a *mortar*.

phonograph: A record player. **Phonographs** aren't as common now that stereos play CDs and tapes.

plaited: To **plait** something is to braid it. My mother **plaited** my sister's hair every morning before school.

prevent: To keep something from happening. A broken leg might **prevent** you from going to gym class.

prowling: To **prowl** is to move secretly or quietly, like an animal hunting its prey. My cat was **prowling** in the backyard, looking for birds to chase.

pullets: Young hens.

quarreling: To **quarrel** is to argue or not agree. The brothers are **quarreling** over whose turn it is to do the dishes.

quivered: To **quiver** is to quickly shake or shiver just a little bit. My stomach **quivered** at the thought of riding the Ferris wheel.

rafters: Long pieces of wood that support the roof of a building.

refreshed: If something makes you feel **refreshed**, it gives you energy and strength again. The tired, sweaty children were **refreshed** by a swim in the pool.

registers: A **register** is a book in which official lists are kept. Teachers sometimes use **registers** to list the students in class and keep track of how many days they have been absent.

relief: You feel **relief** when your worry or pain goes away. It was a great **relief** to wake up feeling better after having the flu for a week.

reprimanding: If someone is **reprimanding** you, that person is speaking to you in an angry way for doing something wrong. The teacher was **reprimanding** the boy for passing notes in class. The girl's father is always **reprimanding** her for slamming the door, but she keeps doing it.

repulsive: Something **repulsive** is very unpleasant or disgusting. There was a **repulsive** smell coming from the trash can, so I took out the trash.

resist: To **resist** is to stay strong against a force or an action. I tried to **resist** the cold by wearing a scarf, a hat, mittens, and two sets of socks.

retorted: When you **retort**, you answer someone quickly, in a mean or clever way. The boy complained about his burned toast, so his sister **retorted** that he should make his own.

revealing: To **reveal** something is to show it or bring it into view. The curtains on the stage lifted, **revealing** the actors in the play.

revived: To **revive** something is to give new strength or life to it. When I felt dizzy on a hot day last summer, a glass of cool water **revived** me.

rhubarb: A plant with very wide leaves and thick red or green stems. You can cook and eat the stems of **rhubarb**, but not the leaves.

roost: To **roost** is to rest or sleep somewhere that a bird might sleep. Birds **roost** in nests, birdhouses, and other places that are built especially for them, like chicken coops. If you curled up in a pile of clothes that looked like a nest, your mother might say you were **roosting**.

rough and ready: Something that is **rough and ready** is useful but not fancy. Old rubber boots are **rough and ready** because they keep your feet dry, even though they aren't good-looking.

salver: A tray for serving food or drinks.

scamp: A **scamp** is someone who causes trouble in a playful way. My friend is such a **scamp**—she hid a frog in my lunchbox last week!

scamper: To **scamper** is to run in a light, quick way. A puppy might **scamper** happily after a ball you throw.

scarcely: Hardly or barely. I slept so late this morning, I **scarcely** had time to get dressed before the bus came.

scold: To **scold** is to speak in a way to show that you are angry or disappointed with someone. He **scolded** his cat for scratching up the couch.

scorching: Something **scorching** is hot enough to burn you. The sand in the desert is **scorching** because the sun beats down on it all day.

scrawny: Skinny and bony. We laughed at the turkeys running around the barnyard on their little **scrawny** legs.

scullion: A **scullion** is a servant who does hard work in a kitchen. The **scullion** peeled carrots, washed all the dishes, and then mopped the kitchen floor.

scurrying: To **scurry** is to move in a hurry. The mouse went **scurrying** into its hole when it saw me coming around the corner.

scythe: A tool that has a curved blade and a long handle, used for cutting grass or crops.

seldom: Not very often. You might **seldom** see your aunt and uncle if they live in another state. We **seldom** go out to dinner at a restaurant because my parents both love to cook.

selfish: If you are **selfish**, you care only about yourself and do not think about or share things with other people. A **selfish** person would never let anyone else play with his or her toys.

señora: Spanish for *Mrs.*

shod: A horse that is **shod** has had horseshoes put on its hooves. People might go to a *blacksmith* (a person who makes things out of iron) to have their horses **shod**.

shrine: A **shrine** is a place created to honor someone. People often pray at a **shrine**, or leave gifts or light candles for the person they are honoring.

sí: Spanish for *yes*.

sidled: To **sidle** is to sneakily move sideways. He **sidled** along the wall to the window and peeked inside the house.

skirting boards: Long pieces of wood placed along the bottom edge of the walls in a house. **Skirting boards** help keep furniture or shoes from making marks on the lower part of the wall.

sneered: To **sneer** is to make a face that shows you dislike something very much or are making fun of it. When you **sneer**, you usually raise one corner of your upper lip. The rude child **sneered** at the teacher and stuck out his tongue.

snobbery: Thinking you are better than everyone else. Your friends might accuse you of **snobbery** if you act like you are smarter than they are.

snubbed: To **snub** someone means that you treat that person without respect or ignore that person. I felt **snubbed** when my friend walked by me in the hall and pretended not to see me. The word **snub** can be used to describe someone's nose. In that case, a **snub nose** is a short nose that turns up a little at the end.

snug: Something **snug** fits very closely or tightly. Last year's clothes might be a little **snug** on you if you've grown.

sombreros: A **sombrero** is a hat with a wide *brim*, which is the edge that sticks out. **Sombreros** are usually made of straw. They are worn in Mexico and the Southwest part of the United States, two places where it is very hot and sunny.

spinster: An old-fashioned word used to describe an older woman who has never been married.

splendor: Great beauty or grandness. The crowd clapped and cheered at the **splendor** of the fireworks display.

squire: An English country gentleman.

stifle: To **stifle** is to feel very sick, or even to die, because you aren't getting enough air to breathe. You should never put a plastic bag over your head because it could make you **stifle**. I feel like I might **stifle** in this terrible summer heat.

strapping: Someone who is **strapping** is big and strong. Wrestlers often have **strapping** bodies.

strolled: To **stroll** is to walk in a slow, relaxed way. I **strolled** down the hall to my classroom since I had plenty of time to get there.

strutted: To **strut** means to walk proudly, usually because you are showing off or trying to impress someone. He **strutted** around the room, showing everyone the medal he won in the science fair.

suited for: To be **suited for** something is to be right for it, or to meet its needs. If you are a good soccer player and a strong leader, you might be **suited for** the job of team captain.

supple: Something **supple** bends and moves easily. Dancers and gymnasts need to have **supple** bodies in order to stretch and leap into the air.

surged: To **surge** is to rush forward with force. At the beach, a wave can **surge** forward suddenly and get you wet. The crowd **surged** forward to get a better view of the stage.

suspicious: When you feel **suspicious**, you don't trust someone because you think the person might be bad or wrong, but you don't have proof. If you think a friend is lying to you but you aren't sure, you might say that you are **suspicious** of him. My sister's guilty look when I asked her where my favorite book was made me **suspicious** that she took it.

swaggered: To **swagger** is to walk in a bold, proud way. The older boy **swaggered** through the playground, daring others to fight him.

swifts: A **swift** is a small dark-colored bird. **Swifts** have long, narrow wings that allow them to fly very fast.

symphony: A long piece of music played by many different instruments. A **symphony** usually has three or four parts, called *movements*. My favorite part of the **symphony** is when the tuba plays.

synthetic: Something **synthetic** is made by humans and is not found in nature. Plastic is an example of a **synthetic** material.

tarry: To **tarry** is to stay in a certain place for a while. In the summertime, you might **tarry** outside for a few more minutes after your mother calls you in for dinner.

tedious: Something **tedious** is tiring because it is boring, slow, or takes a long time. It might be hard to stay awake during a **tedious** movie.

tethering: When you **tether** something, you tie it to something else to keep it in place. The woman climbed out of her boat after **tethering** it to the dock so it wouldn't float away.

thicket: An area where plants, bushes, or small trees are growing very thickly and close together. Small animals and birds often hide themselves in a **thicket**.

tongs: A tool with two arms connected at one end, used for picking things up. **Tongs** are usually made of metal or wood.

trice: When something happens in a **trice**, it happens in a very short amount of time. The ring slipped off her finger in a **trice** and disappeared into the water just as quickly.

tufts: A **tuft** is a bunch of yarn, grass, hair, or feathers that is tied or grows together at one end. Many babies have only little **tufts** of hair on their head when they're born.

uncanny: Something described as **uncanny** is mysterious or strange. The wind was howling in an **uncanny** way, giving the night a spooky feel.

uproar: When things are noisy, exciting, and all mixed up, they are in an **uproar**. There might be an **uproar** on your street if a nearby house is on fire. The fans were in an **uproar** when their baseball team won the championship game.

utmost: Greatest or highest. Since I had very little time to do my chores today, I did only the things of **utmost** importance.

uttered: To **utter** is to speak or to make other sounds with your voice. He **uttered** a shout of pain when someone stepped on his foot.

vain: You are **vain** if you care too much about how you look or are too proud of the things you can do. The **vain** man spent hours staring at himself in the mirror. I am so **vain** about how strong I am, I won't let anyone help me carry heavy boxes.

venturing: To **venture** is putting yourself in danger by doing or saying something bold or risky. If your parents are angry with you for staying up late, you might **venture** to give them an excuse. You could get hurt **venturing** across a busy street during rush hour.

wainscots: A **wainscot** is a panel made of wood that is used to decorate a wall in a house. **Wainscots** may have fancy carvings or designs on them.

wattles: The loose, wrinkled skin hanging down from a turkey's throat.

weave: To **weave** is to make a path through something by moving from side to side or in and out. You might **weave** through a crowd of people to get to the door. To **weave** is also to join or lace thread or yarn together in a pattern to make something, such as cloth.

weft: Woven fabric. The **weft** is made on a *loom* (a machine used for weaving).

whate'er betide ye: An old-fashioned way of saying *whatever happens to you*.

windfall: A piece of sudden good luck that was not expected. The rainstorm was a **windfall** to the farmer whose crops had not gotten enough water for weeks.

wretched: Something **wretched** is made in a poor, sloppy way. My **wretched** umbrella started leaking the minute I went out into the storm.